GRADES PREK-1

101 Content-Building Fingerplays, Action Rhymes, and Songs

Pamela Chanko

New York • Toronto • London • Auckland • Sydney
Mexico City • New Delhi • Hong Kong • Buenos Aires

Teaching *Resources*

For someone whom I'm very glad
I'll always get to call my dad.

The following material was originally written by Pamela Chanko for publication in *Clifford the Big Red Dog* ™ magazine and was adapted by her for this book: *Today's Weather; It's Story Time; One Little Ladybug; My Summer Coat; Dial 911; Fall Has Come to Town; I'll Be Putting on My Mittens; Playful Penguins; Apples & Pumpkins; At the Doctor's; Pets Need Vets!; Help on Thanksgiving;* and *The Perfect Present*.

"Five Little Kites," "Alike & Different," "My Rooster," "The Days of Dinosaurs," and "The Rocketship" from *Biggie Patterns With a Purpose* © 2006 by Pamela Chanko (Scholastic, 2006). Adapted by Pamela Chanko for this publication. Reprinted by permission of Scholastic Inc.

Cover design by Jason Robinson
Interior design by Holly Grundon
Interior illustrations by Maxie Chambliss, Sue Dennen, Kate Flanagan,
James Graham Hale, John Jones, and Anne Kennedy

ISBN-13: 978-0-545-10291-9
ISBN-10: 0-545-10291-X

3 4 5 6 7 8 9 10   40   16 15 14 13 12

Contents

Fingerplays

Contents

Introduction

This little piggy went to market.
This little piggy stayed home.
This little piggy had roast beef.
This little piggy had none.
And this little piggy cried,
"Wee, wee, wee,"
All the way home.

Many of us remember being delighted as children to have our toes or fingers gently tugged while a loved one recited these lines. There was something about the auditory rhythm of the words combined with the physical sensation that created a kind of magic. As children grow, that magic grows with them, and it changes shape and form. Fingerplays (rhymes that include hand movements) and action rhymes (rhymes that incorporate full body movement) help increase memory, build fine and gross motor skills, enhance hand-eye coordination, and improve literacy skills.

One of the most important concepts in literacy learning is that spoken and written language has meaning. When doing the rhyme above, the young child begins to understand that each toe or finger represents one "little piggy," therefore grasping the concept of symbols. And of course, each word in our language is a symbol that carries a specific meaning. When older children engage in fingerplays, they begin associating an action with a word or a series of words, which reinforces the concept that these words convey a particular message. In addition, performing the hand motions helps children improve fine motor skills—which can aid them in their writing.

The rhythm and rhyme inherent in fingerplays and action rhymes is another beneficial aspect of using them with young learners. Children are naturally drawn to the playful, singsong sounds of rhyming words—they are delightful to listen to and fun to say aloud. The more children are exposed to rhymes, the more finely tuned their ears become to the differences between sounds, which helps prepare them for learning the sound-letter associations that are essential for reading. The rhythm of verse is also a great literacy-builder, as it familiarizes children with the natural cadence of language and its musical qualities. In fact, this collection includes some rhymes that are set to the tune of familiar, favorite childhood songs.

You'll find that the fingerplays, rhymes, and songs in this book fit perfectly into your existing schedule and curriculum. And since each takes just a few minutes to recite, you can fit one in anytime!

This delightful collection will help you:

- teach basic concepts (such as alphabet and numbers)

- get more out of circle time and other group activities

- ease transitions throughout the day

- build children's self-concept

- facilitate the development of fine and gross motor skills

- reinforce safety rules

- build the concept of community

- explore favorite themes (such as transportation, animals, and plants)

- celebrate holidays and special occasions

- and much, much more!

You might teach children a rhyme a day or a rhyme a week. You can use the rhymes in this resource in whatever way or order that best suits the needs of your class. For instance, if children need to move around to burn off extra energy, you might engage them in an action rhyme. On a cold, rainy day, you might choose a cheerful fingerplay to perform with children. After all, the verses in this book are meant to be fun. Just remember that these rhymes are not only a way for children to "get their sillies out." Each rhyme can also serve as a valuable stepping stone on a child's road to becoming a great reader and writer. Enjoy!

101 Content-Building Fingerplays, Action Rhymes, and Songs © 2009 by Pamela Chanko, Scholastic Teaching Resources

Tips for Using the Collection

The fingerplays, action rhymes, and songs in this collection can be used "straight out of the box" with children—that is, you can simply read or sing them aloud, demonstrate the movements, and have children follow along. After a few demonstrations, children will probably be able to perform the rhymes on their own or with little direction. You can use the following tips and ideas to help expand children's experiences with the rhymes.

Make a Chart: When sharing a fingerplay, you might write the text (excluding the movement directions) on chart paper and post it at children's eye level. Even if children aren't yet able to read, they'll enjoy exploring letters and words. You can recite the rhyme before introducing the movements. As you read, track the words with your finger. After children are familiar with the words, introduce the movements.

Make a Recording: Record yourself reading aloud several rhymes. Place the recording in a listening center along with copies of the corresponding text. You might also provide illustrations of the movements. Then invite children to visit the center to listen to the rhymes and read along.

Use Props: Many of the rhymes in this collection lend themselves well to being acted out with a few simple props. For instance, children might put magazines, envelopes, and pieces of junk mail in a shoulder bag and use it as a mail sack to act out "Something for the Letter Carrier" (page 85). Or they might make and use construction-paper ladybug stick puppets to perform "One Little Ladybug" (page 32).

Try It Quiet: Once children know the words and movements to a fingerplay, try doing it silently! Lead children in mouthing the words as they perform the hand motions. This is a great activity to do when children need to stay quiet for an extended period, such as waiting in the hallway or auditorium before an assembly.

School-Home Connections: After you teach children a new fingerplay, you might send a copy of the rhyme home with them. Children can teach the words and actions to family members—a great way to involve them in what's going on at school.

Grab-Bag Fun: As children learn new fingerplays, action rhymes, and songs, write the titles on index cards and place them in a paper lunch bag. Whenever you have a few minutes to fill, invite a child to draw a card from the bag. Read the title on the card and have children perform the rhyme!

Sounds and Spellings: Use the rhymes to focus on phonemic awareness and phonics. When reciting a rhyme, take the focus off the movement and ask children to put on their listening caps. For instance, when reading "My Hands" (page 44), ask children to listen for the rhyming words at the ends of the second and fourth lines (*clap, tap*). "The Wind" (page 65) is terrific for teaching sound-spelling patterns, as it contains many rhyming words that are spelled the same way (*day, away, stay, play, say*).

Draw a Rhyme: Children might enjoy illustrating the concepts represented by some of the rhymes. For instance, "When I Grow Up" (page 89) might inspire them to draw self-portraits showing what they would like to do one day. After performing "Mamas and Babies" (page 71), children might create a display showing animal parents with their young.

Perform It: Many of the fingerplays, action rhymes, and songs make great performance pieces for classroom open-houses, holiday parties, or school assemblies. For instance, "The Perfect Present" (page 103) is ideal for a winter holiday program. A performance of "Earth Day Gifts" (page 111) at an assembly might inspire the whole school to "go green" and "give back!" By working with children to create simple backdrops and adding a few props, you'll make each performance an event to remember.

Who's Here?

To take attendance with this chant, insert a child's name in the first verse. Repeat this verse, using a different child's name each time until you've named each child. Then finish the chant. If every child is present, fill in the total number of children in the third verse. If any children are absent, recite *Alternate Verse 3* and fill in the number of children who are present.

_____, _____, what do you say?
Raise your hand if you're here today!

(Child raises hand.)

Wave to your friends,

(Child waves to group.)

And they'll wave to you.

(Group waves back.)

That is just what good friends do!

Children, children, what do you say?
Let's count who is here today!

(Point to each child as you count.)

That's _____ children, give a cheer
'Cause every one of us is here!

(Raise fist in cheering motion.)

Alternate Verse 3:

That's _____ children, that's
   too bad—
We're not all here, but don't be sad!
We miss the friends who aren't here,
But they'll be back, so give a cheer!

(Raise fist in cheering motion.)

Morning Welcome Song

(Sing to the tune of "Have You Ever Seen a Lassie?")

Welcome children to school with this catchy tune. Choose the appropriate second verse to sing according to the following: *Version 1* on regular weekdays, *Version 2* when returning to school after a weekend, and *Version 3* when returning after a vacation or holiday. Wave to a different child each time you sing "Good morning."

Oh, let's all wave good morning,
Good morning, good morning.
   (Wave to children.)
Oh, let's all wave good morning,
Good morning to you!
   (Wave to children.)

Version 1:

We slept all last night,
   (Rest head on hands.)
Let's start the day right,
   (Give two "thumbs-up" signs.)
Oh, let's all wave good morning,
Good morning to you.
   (Wave to children.)

Morning Welcome Song

(continued)

Version 2:

After two days away,

(Hold up two fingers.)

We've so much to say,

(Make "talk" motion with hand.)

Oh, let's all wave good morning,

Good morning to you.

(Wave to children.)

Note: After an extended weekend, you can replace the word *two* with the appropriate number of days, such as *three* or *four*.

Version 3:

Our time off was cool,

(Make "OK" sign with thumb and index finger.)

Now we're back at school,

(Clap hands.)

Oh, let's all wave good morning,

Good morning to you.

(Wave to children.)

Today's Weather

(Sing to the tune of "Twinkle, Twinkle, Little Star")

Sing this song to enhance two daily routines: marking the calendar and reporting the weather. Insert a child's name in the fifth line of each verse.

What's the date and what's the day?

(Shrug, palms up.)

Look up here—what do you say?

(Point to calendar.)

What's the month and what's the year?

The calendar should make it clear.

_____, tell us right away,

(Point to named child.)

What's the date and what's the day?

(Scratch head as if thinking.)

What's the weather like today?

(Shrug, palms up.)

Look outside—what do you say?

(Point to window.)

Is it chilly, is it warm?

Is it windy, will it storm?

_____, tell us right away,

(Point to named child.)

What's the weather like today?

(Scratch head as if thinking.)

Circle Time Choo-Choo

Use this rhyme to gather children for circle time. Begin a train by chugging around the room. Recite the first verse, inserting the same child's name in each of the blanks. Repeat the verse, each time using a different child's name. As children are called, have them "hook" onto the train by holding onto the person in front of them. When only one child is left, recite the last verse, using that child's name in the blank. Then guide the train to the circle time area and have children sit down.

First Verse:

_____, _____, that's your name,
Come and join our choo-choo train.
The choo-choo train is going far,
And now we have another car!
Our friend _____ has joined the train.
It's time to call another name!

Last Verse:

Our friend _____ has joined the train,
And there are no more names to name!
Now everyone has joined the fun.
At last, our choo-choo train is done!
We chugged around and said this rhyme
And now we'll stop for circle time!

Who's Who?

(Sing to the tune of "The Farmer in the Dell")

Sing this getting-to-know-you song to help children introduce themselves and share the activities they enjoy. Sing the first verse and invite a child to respond. Then use that child's name and response in the second verse, pantomiming the action for the named activity (for example, "Oh, Peter likes to paint"). Repeat the song until each child has been named and has had a turn to name a favorite activity.

Our classroom is brand new,
Let's see just who is who,
We'll play a game,
Just say your name
And what you like to do.
(Point out a child who will then introduce
himself and name a favorite activity.)

Oh, _____ likes to _____,
Oh, _____ likes to _____,
(Pretend to do the activity.)
And some of you
May like it, too.
(Point around circle.)
Oh _____ likes to _____.
(Pretend to do the activity.)

Cool School Rules

Use this fingerplay at circle time or anytime to review important rules.

I raise my hand before I talk.

(Raise hand.)

I watch for others when I walk.

(Shield eyes with hand and look from side to side.)

Outside, I get to run around.

(Pump arms quickly.)

Inside, I try to keep it down.

(Put finger to lips.)

I listen to what teachers say.

(Cup hand behind ear.)

I pledge to do my best each day.

(Put hand over heart.)

When everybody follows rules,

(Sweep arms out, indicating everyone.)

We all have lots of fun at school!

(Clap.)

Getting Centered

Use this fingerplay to get children excited about center time—or simply a day of possibilities!

If I want to paint a picture,
There's a center just for Art.
(Pretend to paint with brush.)

In Blocks, I build a tower,
(Pretend to stack blocks.)
Then I take it all apart.
(Pretend to remove one block at a time.)

If I want to cook some dinner,
I can do Dramatic Play.
(Pretend to stir food in a pan.)

The Math Center is handy
If there's something I must weigh.
*(With both palms facing up, alternate moving
one hand up and the other down, as if balancing a scale.)*

The Language Center's always there
For me to write or read.
(Pretend to write on palm of hand.)

Whatever I may want to do,
My class has what I need!
(Hold arms out.)

Clean-Up Time

(Sing to the tune of "I've Been Working on the Railroad")

Use this tune to get children ready to clean up after center time.

Time for cleaning up my center,

(Pretend to sweep.)

Putting things away.

Time for cleaning up my center,

(Pretend to wipe table with sponge.)

So someone else can play.

When my center's neat and tidy,

(Make "OK" sing with thumb and index finger.)

Everyone will see,

I can help to make the classroom

(Point to self.)

A nicer place to be!

(Spread arms.)

Line-Up Marching Song

(Sing to the tune of "Do Your Ears Hang Low?")

Sing this song several times as you call children to line up.

Come and line up straight.

(Children join line.)

Shoulders back, you're looking great.

(Arch shoulders back, chest out.)

Put your hands down at your sides.

(Put hands at sides.)

Seal your lips, we won't be late.

(Press lips tightly together.)

Put your chin up high and proud.

(Stick up chin.)

In the hallway, don't be loud.

(Shake head.)

Are you lined up straight?

(Nod head.)

From the Outside In!

(Sing to the tune of "When the Saints Go Marching In")

Use this song to get children ready to come back inside after recess.

Oh, when it's time to go back in,
Oh, when it's time to go back in,
We shake out the rest of our sillies,
　(Shake and jiggle.)
When it's time to go back in.

Oh, when it's time to go indoors,
Oh, when it's time to go indoors,
We brush off the dirt from the outdoors,
　(Pretend to brush off clothes.)
When it's time to go indoors.

Oh, when it's time to go inside,
Oh, when it's time to go inside,
We line up, one after the other,
　(Form a line.)
When it's time to go inside.

Oh, now we're set to go back in,
Oh, now we're set to go back in,
We are calm and ready and quiet,
　(Put finger to lips and whisper-sing.)
And we're about to go back in!

Scrub, Rub-a-Dub

Recite this rhyme with children who are waiting in line to wash their hands at the sink.

Ten little fingers,
What a sight to see.

(Wiggle ten fingers.)

Two little palms,
Just dirty as can be!

(Look at palms and frown.)

Two little wrists
That really need a wash.

(Rub wrists together as if scrubbing.)

Ten little nails
Need scrubbing, oh my gosh!

(Look at fingernails.)

Scrub, rub-a-dub,
It's like a little game.

(Rub hands together.)

Add soap and water—
Germs go down the drain!

*(Point down with index finger,
making spiral motion.)*

Snack Song

(Sing to the tune of "Are You Sleeping?")

Use this song to get children to the table for snack time.

Are you hungry, are you hungry,

(Rub tummy.)

For a snack? For a snack?

(Put fingers to mouth and pretend to eat.)

It's the time to eat now.

(Tap wrist as if touching watch.)

Stop and have a treat now.

(Hold palm out to indicate "stop.")

Yum, yum, yum! Yum, yum, yum!

(Clap on each "yum.")

Jiggle, Wiggle, and Giggle

Use this movement poem during any transition time to help children get their "sillies" out. Simply have children perform the actions mentioned in the rhyme. At the end, have them sit for circle time, story time, or any other activity.

It's time to get our sillies out,
So come and join the fun.
We're getting all the giggles out,
We'll wiggle 'til we're done!

Roll your head in circles,
Then flop it side to side.
Now jiggle both your shoulders,
And stretch your arms up high.

Wiggle all your fingers.
Give your ears a tug.
Twist your waist, bend back and forth,
And give yourself a hug!

Wiggle all your toes-ies,
Then gently run in place.
Stick your tongue out all the way,
And make a silly face!

Wiggle, jiggle every part.
Be a silly clown!
Now take a breath . . . and let it out.
(Take deep breath, then exhale slowly.)
It's time to settle down.

101 Content-Building Fingerplays, Action Rhymes, and Songs © 2009 by Pamela Chanko, Scholastic Teaching Resources

It's Story Time

Use this fingerplay when previewing a book with a picture walk. As you recite the words, have children perform the hand motions in the second verse. Then display the book as indicated in the third verse.

It's story time,
So gather 'round.
Come see the book
That I just found.

Your ears are to listen,
(Cup hands behind ears.)
Your eyes are to look.
(Form circles around eyes with
thumbs and index fingers.)
So let's get together
And read a great book!

Here is the book,
(Point to book.)
And this is the cover.
(Display cover of book.)
When we open it up,
(Open book.)
There's a lot to discover!
(Display pages to children.)

The Lunchbox

Use this rhyme to transition into or out of lunchtime.

I wish I could open my lunchbox

(Pretend to open lunchbox lid.)

To something exciting and new.

(Put hands on cheeks to show surprise.)

I wish I could spy a whole pizza pie,

(Hold arms out in front to form a circle.)

Or a big pot of hamburger stew!

(Pretend to stir stew with both hands.)

Well, maybe fried eggs would be smelly,

(Pinch nose.)

And maybe spaghetti would leak,

*(Hold up both hands and look down at lap,
as if something has spilled.)*

But, oh! Peanut butter and jelly

(Press palms together to make a "sandwich.")

Gets boring each day of the week!

*(Open hands as if opening sandwich
and frown.)*

101 Content-Building Fingerplays, Action Rhymes, and Songs © 2009 by Pamela Chanko, Scholastic Teaching Resources

Counting Sheep

Use this rhyme as a quiet activity for children who don't nap during rest time. Recite the rhyme in a soft whisper and let children count the sheep by raising one finger at a time.

It's rest time—if you're not asleep,
Shhh . . . let's whisper; let's count sheep.

One small sheep curls up in bed;
Another rests its sleepy head.

One turns out the bedside light;
Another says, "Goodnight, sleep tight."

One sheep hugs a teddy bear;
Another breathes the cool night air.

One sheep sighs a peaceful sigh;
Another hums a lullaby.

One can stay awake no more,
And one last sheep begins to snore.

We counted sheep from one to ten.
Still awake? Then count again.

But this time, count them in your head—
Don't wake the sheep; they're all in bed!

Show and Tell

This special rhyme serves as a gentle reminder to children
of the importance of paying attention to others.

Show and tell is special,

(Clap hands together once.)

An exciting time of day.

(Rub hands back and forth.)

It's when my friends bring things from home,

Or maybe far away.

I use my ears to listen.

(Point to ears.)

I use my eyes to see.

(Point to eyes.)

I always pay attention,

(Sit up straight, shoulders back.)

As I know they would for me!

(Point to self with thumbs.)

So-Long Song

(Sing to the tune of "The Itsy-Bitsy Spider")

Seat children in a circle and sing this song to wrap up the school day.

A very special classroom

　(Point around circle to indicate whole class.)

Had a busy day.

　(Pump arms as if walking.)

They had lots to learn,

　(Point to head.)

And lots of time to play.

　(Clap hands as if playing pat-a-cake.)

Now the day is over,

　(Frown.)

They'll all go home and then

　("Walk" two fingers along other arm.)

That very special classroom

　(Point around circle to indicate whole class.)

Will do it all again!

　(Clap.)

The Letter Cheer

Use this fingerplay to reinforce any letter of the alphabet—simply fill in the first and third blanks with the letter of your choice. Use the sound of the letter in the second blank. Perform the rhyme near an alphabet frieze, or display a set of alphabet cards so children can point to the appropriate letter.

Letter ____,
Let's give a cheer,

   (Raise fist in cheering motion.)

It makes the ____ sound,
Can you hear?

   (Cup hand behind ear.)

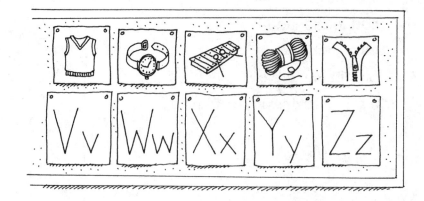

Let's point to ____
Right over there.

   (Point to letter.)

And now let's draw it
In the air!

   (Draw letter in air with index finger.)

The Vowel Song

(Sing to the tune of "Bingo")

As you sing this song, clap once for each missing letter. Perform the song near an alphabet frieze or display letter cards, so that you or a volunteer can point to the missing letters in each verse.

Our alphabet, it has five vowels.
They're very special letters—
A, E, I, O, U.
A, E, I, O, U.
A, E, I, O, U.
They make our words sound better!

These vowels, they can be short or long.
They're very special letters—
__, E, I, O, U.
__, E, I, O, U.
__, E, I, O, U.
They make our words sound better!

The long vowels sound just like their names.
They're very special letters—
__, __, I, O, U.
__, __, I, O, U.
__, __, I, O, U.
They make our words sound better!

At least one vowel's in every word.
They're very special letters—
__, __, __, O, U.
__, __, __, O, U.
__, __, __, O, U.
They make our words sound better!

Vowels can sometimes work in pairs.
They're very special letters—
__, __, __, __, U.
__, __, __, __, U.
__, __, __, __, U.
They make our words sound better!

So now you know a song of vowels.
They're very special letters—
__, __, __, __, __.
__, __, __, __, __.
__, __, __, __, __.
They make our words sound better!

Adjective Alphabet

Recite this rhyme to teach letters as well as descriptive words. Post a copy of the Alphabet Hand Signs chart nearby for children to use as a reference when forming each letter. You might also have children make up an action to perform for each adjective in the rhyme.

A is for awesome,
B is for busy.
C is for careful,
D is for dizzy!

E is for excellent,
F is for flappy.
G is for grumpy,
H is for happy!

I is for interesting,
J is for jumpy.
K is for kind,
L is for lumpy!

M is for magical,
N is for nice.
O is for orange,
P's for precise.

Q is for quiet,
R is for rusty.
S is for special,
T is for trusty.

U's for unusual,
V is for vexed.
W's for wild,
X is for x'ed!

Y is for yellow,
Z is for zany.
I know all my letters—
Which means I am brainy!

Alphabet Hand Signs

	A	B	C	
D	E	F	G	H
I	J	K	L	M
N	O	P	Q	R
S	T	U	V	W
	X	Y	Z	

One Little Ladybug

To count the ladybugs in this rhyme, raise and wiggle
the number of fingers named in each verse.

One little ladybug,
Playing peek-a-boo,
Along came another,
And then there were two.

Two little ladybugs
Share a cup of tea.
Along came another,
And then there were three.

Three little ladybugs
Going to the store,
Along came another,
And then there were four.

Four little ladybugs
Going for a drive,
Along came another,
And then there were five.

Five little ladybugs
Had a busy day.
So they all wave goodbye.
   (Wave hand.)
And they all crawl away!
   *(Wiggle fingers while moving
   hand behind back.)*

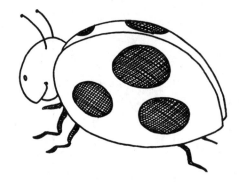

Five Little Kites

Begin this countdown rhyme with all five fingers of one hand raised.
Bend down one finger at a time to subtract each kite.

Five little kites
When it started to pour.
Take one down,
And now there are four.

Four little kites,
One stuck in a tree.
Take one down,
And now there are three.

Three little kites
When a strong wind blew.
Take one down,
And now there are two.

Two little kites,
One's tail came undone.
Take one down,
And then there is one.

One little kite
Flying far, far away.
("Fly" one finger into air,
then behind back.)
No more kites
In the sky today!
(Shake head.)

Color Surprise

Use this rhyme to help children learn colors and associate them with objects around them.

Red is the ladybug
There in the grass.

*("Crawl" two fingers across
palm of other hand.)*

Orange is orange juice
Poured in a glass.

*(Pretend to hold glass in one hand
and pour with the other.)*

Yellow's the sun,
So high in the sky.

(Hold arms over head in a circle.)

Green is the frog
Who's catching a fly.

(Pretend to catch a fly in the air.)

Blue is the bluebird
Who's saying "tweet, tweet."

(Flap arms like wings.)

Purple is violets
That smell very sweet.

(Pretend to sniff a bouquet of flowers.)

Put them all in a row
And then what do I see?

(Shield brow.)

A beautiful rainbow
For you and for me!

(Point out and then back to self.)

Shapes All Around

As you name each shape in this rhyme, lead children in drawing the shape in the air.
As an alternative, children might hold up or point to pictures of the shapes. Use the last line of the
rhyme to encourage children to look for more shapes around your classroom or outdoors.

A circle—that's the big bright sun,
Shining down on everyone.

A square—why, that's a window pane,
And every side is just the same.

A triangle's a pizza slice,
Or apple pie is also nice.

A diamond—that's a kite so high,
Flying in the big blue sky.

A rectangle's our classroom door.
Shapes all around—let's find some more!

L Is for Left!

Use this rhyme to help children learn to tell their left from their right hand.

Though both my hands may look the same,
Each one has a different name.

(Hold up hands and examine them.)

Right or left? Oh golly gee,
The difference can be hard to see!

(Press palms to cheeks and look worried.)

But here's how I can always tell:

*(Hold up both hands, with palms facing out
and thumbs touching each other.)*

My left hand makes the letter *L*!

*(Fold down last three fingers on both
hands to form an "L" and a backward "L.")*

Big and Little

Reinforce the size concepts of *big* and *little* with this fun rhyme. As you recite the rhyme, use the corresponding hand positions for the boldface words, shown below.

big and **enormous**

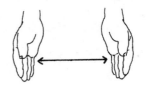

Standing near an insect,
I look very **big** and **tall**.
But put me near an elephant,
And suddenly I'm **small**.

tall

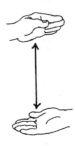

A mouse is really **tiny**,
That's very plain to see.
But that mouse looks just **enormous**
When you put it near a flea.

small

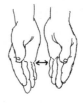

There are many different sizes.
You may think you know them all.
   (Point finger to head as if thinking.)
But then look at who you're next to—
You might be both **big** and **small**!

tiny

Two Little Birds

Perform this fingerplay to help children learn about opposites.

Two little birds, sitting in a tree.
*(Form two beaks facing each other
with hands.)*
Two little birds, who couldn't agree!
*(Shake beaks back and forth to
indicate "no.")*

When one said "up,"
(Point up.)
The other said "down."
(Point down.)

When one would smile,
(Smile.)
The other would frown.
(Frown.)

When one said "hot,"
(Wipe brow with hand.)
The other said "cold."
(Hug self and shiver.)

When one said "young,"
(Pretend to rock baby in arms.)
The other said "old."
(Pretend to stroke long beard.)

When one said "right,"
(Make "thumbs-up" sign.)
The other said "wrong."
(Make "thumbs-down" sign.)

When one said "short,"
(Hold hands a short distance apart.)
The other said "long."
(Spread hands a long distance apart.)

Two little birds, sitting in a tree.
*(Form two beaks facing each other
with hands.)*
Two little birds, will they ever agree?
(Hold palms up and shrug shoulders.)

Weekday Warm-Up!

Use this high-energy action rhyme to give children practice in naming the days of the week.

Seven days are in a week.
That's seven days to play.

(Hold up seven fingers.)

Seven different ways to move—
One for every day!

(Hold up one finger.)

Mondays are for marching.

(March in place.)

Tuesdays are for tiptoeing.

(Tiptoe in place.)

Wednesdays are for waving.

(Wave arms.)

Thursdays are for thumping.

(Thump one foot on floor.)

Fridays are for flapping.

(Flap arms like wings.)

Saturdays are for stretching.

(Stretch up.)

Sundays are for skipping.

(Skip in place.)

Seven different ways to move,
Seven ways to play.

(Hold up seven fingers.)

Now, tell me by the way you move—
What day is it today?

*(Perform the action for the appropriate
day of the week.)*

A Year of Months

Children perform actions that go with each month of the year with this clever rhyme.

In January it may snow.

*(Flutter fingers down
to represent falling snow.)*

In February, cold winds blow.

(Hug self and shiver.)

In March, a kite is flying high.

(Point up to sky.)

In April, rain clouds fill the sky.

*(Reach arms up and out
as if holding a cloud.)*

In May, the seeds begin to sprout.

(Point to ground.)

In June, the insects crawl about.

*("Crawl" two fingers across
palm of other hand.)*

A Year of Months

(continued)

July is when the sun shines bright.

(Hold arms in a circle over head.)

In August, stars light up the night.

*(Open and close fingers quickly
in flashing motion.)*

September means it's back to school.

(March in place.)

October means the air gets cool.

(Rub hands together.)

We rake November leaves, and then

(Pretend to rake leaves.)

December—it gets cold again!

(Hug self and shiver.)

Me and My Clock

Use this rhyme to practice telling time. You might make a large clock face—
with numbers but no hands—to display on a wall. Invite children to stand in front of the clock
to perform the rhyme, using their arms as the hands on the clock. On the last verse,
position a volunteer's arms to "set" the clock and have children tell the time.

I have a clock that has a face.

(Point to face.)

It doesn't look like mine.

(Shake head.)

The face has numbers on it,
And they help to tell the time.

(Point to wrist as if touching a watch.)

My clock, it also has two hands.

(Hold out hands.)

They're not like mine at all.

(Shake head.)

One of them is big and long,

(Stretch arms out wide.)

The other short and small.

(Move arms closer in.)

The small hand tells the hour,

(Hold right arm out to side and point finger.)

As the big hand moves around.

(Point left finger and move arm in a circle.)

The big hand tells the minutes,
And it makes a ticking sound.

My hands can act just like a clock's,
Though I don't tock or chime.
My big hand's here,

(Point left arm to any position.)

My small one's there—

(Point right arm to any position.)

Now can you guess the time?

(Group guesses time being represented.)

101 Content-Building Fingerplays, Action Rhymes, and Songs © 2009 by Pamela Chanko, Scholastic Teaching Resources

You Can Count on Me!

Reinforce body awareness with this delightful rhyme.

Here are my ten wiggly fingers, *(Wiggle fingers.)*

And here are my ten tiny toes. *(Wiggle toes.)*

Here are my two big strong arms, *(Flex biceps.)*

And here is my one little nose. *(Point to nose.)*

Here are my two funny elbows, *(Show elbows.)*

And here are my two floppy feet. *(Point to feet.)*

Here are my thousands of hairs, *(Touch hair.)*

And who knows what number of teeth. *(Point to teeth.)*

What do these parts all add up to? *(Scratch head, thinking.)*

Just do the addition and see.

When you put all those numbers together,

They add up to one special me!
*(Hold up one finger on one hand and point to self
with thumb of other hand.)*

My Hands

With this rhyme, children discover many different ways they can use their hands.

My hands can reach.

(Reach hands up in the air.)

My hands can clap.

(Clap hands together.)

My hands can draw.

(Pretend to draw on table or floor.)

My hands can tap.

(Tap hands on thighs.)

My hands can stir
To help you cook.

(Pretend to stir with both hands.)

They turn the pages
Of a book.

*(Pretend to hold book
and turn pages.)*

My hands can paint.

(Pretend to paint.)

My hands can write.

(Pretend to write on palm.)

My hands can touch,

(Touch fingertips together.)

But never fight.

*(Put hands behind back and
shake head "no.")*

My hands can do so much,
You see—

(Hold arms out, smile.)

I'm glad they are
Attached to me!

(Point at self with both thumbs.)

Super Senses

Use this rhyme to teach children about the five senses.

My nose is there to help me smell.

(Point to nose.)

My ears can help me hear a bell.

(Cup hands behind ears.)

My fingers help me touch and feel.

(Wiggle fingers.)

My mouth can taste a yummy meal.

(Point to mouth.)

My eyes are there to look about.

(Shield brow with hand and look around.)

My senses help me find things out!

(Point to head.)

My Feelings and Me

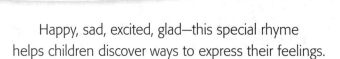

Happy, sad, excited, glad—this special rhyme
helps children discover ways to express their feelings.

I cry when I am very sad.

(Rotate fists in front of eyes as if crying.)

I stamp my foot when I am mad.

(Stamp foot.)

Excitement sometimes makes me jump.

(Jump up.)

When I feel bad, my shoulders slump.

(Hang head and slump shoulders.)

Sometimes I feel very shy,

(Hide face behind hands.)

But then I laugh and don't know why!

(Hold belly and shake.)

I show my feelings, 'cause you see,

(Hold arms out.)

My feelings are a part of me!

(Hug self.)

The Child in the Mirror

Help build children's self-awareness with this action rhyme. You might have children perform the rhyme in front of a wall mirror. If you do this, when children reach the first part of the last verse, have them point to themselves in the mirror instead of doing the described action.

When I look in the mirror,

Here's what I see: *(Shield brow.)*

The one other person *(Hold up one finger.)*

Who looks just like me. *(Point to self.)*

This person is funny, *(Hold belly and shake.)*

And also is smart. *(Point to head.)*

This person is friendly, *(Shake hands with self.)*

And has a good heart. *(Place hands on heart.)*

This person is someone

I really like seeing— *(Shield brow, nod, and smile.)*

Because it's a person

I really like being! *(Hug self.)*

Alike and Different

(Sing to the tune of "This Old Man")

Have children sit or stand in a circle as they sing this uplifting song
about their similarities and differences.

You are you,

   (Point to a person in the circle.)

I am me,

   (Point to self.)

We are different,

Can't you see?

   (Continue pointing back and forth.)

Different eyes,

   (Point to eyes.)

Different hair,

   (Point to hair.)

Different voice to sing a song,

   (Point to throat.)

But we still can get along.

   (Clap.)

I'm like you,

   (Point to self.)

You're like me,

   (Point to someone else in the circle.)

We're alike,

Oh, can't you see?

   (Continue pointing back and forth.)

We can laugh,

   (Hold belly and shake.)

We can love,

   (Put hands on heart.)

We can play and we can share,

   (Put arms across neighbors' shoulders.)

Just like children everywhere!

   (Sway back and forth.)

All Kinds of Families

Use this rhyme to help develop children's understanding of families.

Some families are very big,

(Spread arms wide.)

And some are very small.

(Bring hands closer together.)

Some kids have lots of siblings,

(Pretend to count off on fingers.)

And some have none at all.

(Cross hands with palms down, then sweep apart.)

Some families have two parents,

(Hold up two fingers.)

And some have only one.

(Hold up one finger.)

There are lots of combinations

(Hold out one palm.)

When all is said and done.

(Hold out other palm.)

Every family is different,

(Keep both palms out.)

And it's not like any other.

(Shake head.)

So what makes it a family?

(Shrug shoulders, palms still out.)

They all love one another!

(Hug self.)

I Can Share

(Sing to the tune of "Hush Little Baby")

Invite children to find a partner to sing this song with.
Have them switch partners each time they repeat the song.

If I had a yummy treat,

    (Rub tummy.)

I would give you some to eat.

    (Hold out cupped hands.)

And if I had a brand new book,

    (Press palms together to make a "book.")

I would let you come and look.

    (Open hands as if opening book.)

And if you had some work to do,

    *(Move one hand in circles as if
    washing a window.)*

I'd help you out and share that, too.

    *(Continue motion with first hand
    and join in with other hand.)*

And if I had a whole free day,

    (Spread arms wide.)

We'd share it and we'd laugh and play.

    (Clap hands as if playing pat-a-cake.)

But if I had a nasty flu,

    (Pretend to sneeze.)

That I would NOT share with you!

    (Push both arms out and shake head.)

Signs of Good Manners

Use this call-and-response fingerplay to teach children the American Sign Language (ASL) hand signs for four polite phrases.

What's the perfect thing to say
If someone's standing in your way?
Excuse me!

(Hold left palm up, then stroke palm away from self with fingertips of right hand.)

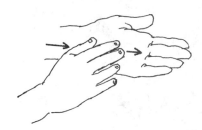

If someone passes you a snack,
Tell me, what do you say back?
Thank you!

(Place fingertips on lips, then tip forward, like blowing a kiss.)

What's the word that can't be beat
If you want a special treat?
Please!

(Rub right palm on chest in a circle.)

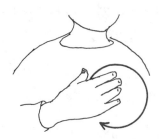

If you step on someone's toe,
What's a way to say, "Oh no"?
I'm sorry!

(Rub right fist on chest in a circle.)

Did you get the answers right?
(Nod head.)
You know how to be polite!

If You're Healthy and You Know It

(Sing to the tune of "If You're Happy and You Know It")

Highlight healthy habits with this catchy song. Each time you sing the following phrases, have children perform these corresponding actions: "Brush, brush!"—pretend to brush teeth; "Wash, wash!"—pretend to wash hands; and "Zzzz, zzzz!"—rest head on hands as if pretending to sleep.

If you're healthy and you know it,
Brush your teeth. Brush, brush!

If you're healthy and you know it,
Brush your teeth. Brush, brush!

If you're healthy and you know it,

And you really want to show it,

If you're healthy and you know it,
Brush your teeth. Brush, brush!

If you're healthy and you know it,
Wash your hands. Wash, wash!

If you're healthy and you know it,
Wash your hands. Wash, wash!

If you're healthy and you know it,

And you really want to show it,

If you're healthy and you know it,
Wash your hands. Wash, wash!

If you're healthy and you know it,
Get your rest. *Zzzz, zzzz!*

If you're healthy and you know it,
Get your rest. *Zzzz, zzzz!*

If you're healthy and you know it,

And you really want to show it,

If you're healthy and you know it,
Get your rest. *Zzzz, zzzz!*

A Hearty Workout

This lively action rhyme is a perfect way to teach children about heart-healthy exercise.

Everybody, run, run, run!
Your heart is having lots of fun!
(Run in place.)

Everybody, jump, jump, jump!
Your heart beats faster—hear it thump!
(Jump in place.)

Everybody, move those feet!
Hear your heart go beat, beat, beat!
(Dance around in a circle.)

Everybody, march in place.
Now your heart will end its race.
(March in place, beginning to cool down.)

Keep on marching—now go slower.
Feel your pulse as it gets lower.
(Place fingers on wrist.)

To help your heart to do its best,
Speed it up, then take a rest.
(Thump fist on chest over heart.)

Now, give your heart a healthy day
Just by going out to play!
(Jump up and cheer.)

In the Bathtub

(Sing to the tune of "Take Me Out to the Ball Game")

Sing this delightful song to remind children of the importance of taking a bath.

Get me into the bathtub,
   (Pretend to climb into tub and sit.)
Let me bring my shampoo,
   (Pretend to wash hair.)

Give me some soap, turn the water on,
   (Pretend to take a bath, continuing for next three lines.)
Pretty soon all the dirt will be gone!

With the scrub, scrub, scrub
   of my washcloth,
I'm getting clean as can be,

And then splash!
   (Pretend to hop out of tub and stand up.)
I'm out of the tub—
I'm a brand new me!
   (Hold arms out and smile.)

My Summer Coat

Perform this cute rhyme to help reinforce the importance of wearing sunscreen.

In summer, when the weather's hot,

(Wipe brow.)

I do not need my gloves.

*(Shake head and pretend
to take off gloves.)*

I do not need my sweater

(Pretend to pull off sweater.)

When the sun shines high above!

(Shield eyes, squint, and point up.)

I do not need my jacket,

(Pretend to take off jacket.)

Or my fuzzy winter hat.

(Pretend to take off hat.)

But every day I wear a coat —

(Hold up one index finger.)

Are you surprised at that?

*(Place hands on cheeks,
make surprised face.)*

No matter where I'm going,

(Wag index finger back and forth.)

To the beach or on a boat,

(Hold up one palm, then the other.)

I always put my sunscreen on—

(Pretend to rub sunscreen on arms.)

'Cause that's my summer coat!

(Hold arms out and smile.)

Safe Little Monkeys

Recite this rhyme to the rhythm of "Five Little Monkeys Jumping on the Bed."
Hold up the number of fingers indicated in the first line of each verse.

Five little monkeys,
Riding on their bikes.
One without a helmet,
Which Mama didn't like.
Mama called the doctor,
And the doctor said, "Yikes!
Monkeys must be safe
When riding on their bikes!"

Four little monkeys,
Riding in a van.
One rode without a seatbelt—
A very careless plan.
Mama called the doctor,
And the doctor said, "Man!
Monkeys must be safe
When riding in a van!"

Three little monkeys,
All about to sneeze.
One didn't use a tissue,
And mama wasn't pleased.
Mama called the doctor,
And the doctor said, "Jeez!
Monkeys must be safe
When they're about to sneeze!"

Two little monkeys,
Going for a skate.
One without his kneepads,
Let's hope it's not too late!
Mama called the doctor,
And the doctor said, "Wait!
Monkeys must be safe
When they're going for a skate!"

One little monkey
Crossed the street to play.
But before the monkey crossed,
He didn't look both ways.
Mama called the doctor,
And the doctor said, "Hey!
Monkeys must be safe
When they cross the street to play!"

Now all the little monkeys
(Frown and shake fist.)
Were feeling very down.
No little monkeys
Were going into town.
Mama called the doctor
And he said, "Don't frown!
Safe little monkeys
Can still monkey around!"

(Smile and wiggle fingers.)

The Traffic Light

Red, green, and yellow—use this fingerplay to teach children what these traffic light colors mean.

Red means stop.

(Push out both hands, palms facing out.)

Green means go.

(Point both index fingers forward.)

Yellow means to take it slow.

(Rotate fists slowly in a circle.)

In a car,

(Pretend to steer wheel.)

On a bike,

(Pretend to hold handlebars.)

If you're going on a hike,

(Pump arms as if walking.)

Play it safe.

(Cross arms across chest.)

Do it right.

(Give two "thumbs-up.")

Always watch the traffic light!

(Point to both eyes, then point out.)

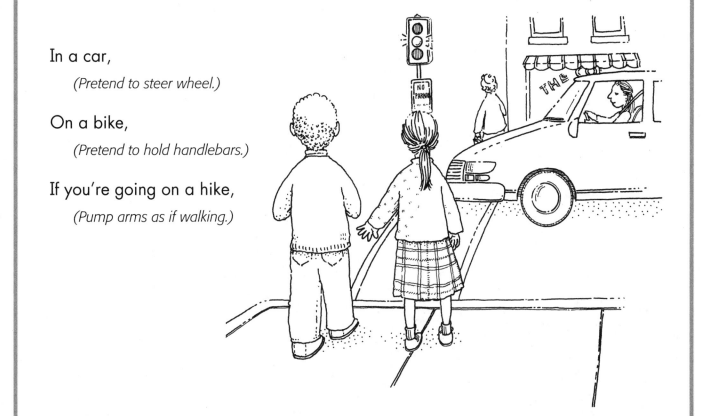

Stop, Drop, and Roll!

Children learn an important safety rule with this action rhyme.

If your clothes catch on fire,
Don't run or hop!
There are three things to do,
And the first one is . . .
STOP!

(Freeze in place.)

If you want to stay safe,
Don't flip or flop!
The next step is easy—
Just get down and . . .
DROP!

(Drop to the ground.)

Remember these steps
If safety's your goal.
Now that you're down,
The last step is to . . .
ROLL!

(Roll back and forth.)

Dial 911

Help children learn this rhyme as a reminder of what number to call in an emergency.

Hold up ten fingers,

(Hold up all fingers on both hands.)

Make one disappear,

(Put down thumb of right hand.)

First, push the *nine*

When danger is near.

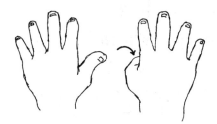

Hold up one hand,

(Hold up all fingers on left hand.)

Put four fingers away,

(Put down all fingers of left hand

except index finger.)

Next comes a *one*

For saving the day!

Hold up one finger,

(Hold up index finger of right hand.)

So straight and so tall.

Now, push the *one*

To finish the call!

A Tree for All Seasons

Use this fingerplay to describe how a tree changes from season to season.
Have children perform the actions shown for each season.

My tree is my friend,
And here is the reason:

(Press hands to chest.)

My tree may not talk,
But it tells me the season!

(Pretend to "zip" lips.)

My tree says it's winter
With limbs that are bare.

(Pretend to be a tree. See 1 below.)

When its buds start to open,
Then spring's in the air.

*(Cradle fist in other hand, then slowly
open fingers. See 2 below.)*

My tree says it's summer
With fruit that hangs down.

(Pretend to pick fruit. See 3 below.)

Then it tells me it's autumn
With leaves on the ground.

(Flutter fingers down. See 4 below.)

My tree doesn't speak;
It does not make a sound—

(Put finger to lips and shake head.)

But it still gives me messages
All the year 'round!

*(Hold hands out, then bring them in
toward self while nodding head.)*

1. winter

2. spring

3. summer

4. fall

Winter's Here

(Sing to the tune of "Jingle Bells")

Sing about the joys of winter while performing the actions to this cheerful tune.

Winter's here, winter's here,
Let's go out to play!
   (Clap.)
Grab some snow and make a ball,
   (Pretend to make a snowball.)
Then send it on its way, hey!
   (Pretend to throw snowball.)

We can ski, we can skate,
   (Pretend to ski and skate.)
A chill is in the air!
   (Hug self and shiver.)
Then when we go back inside,
Hot cocoa's what we'll share!
   (Pretend to sip cup of hot cocoa.)

Winter's here, winter's here,
The snow is falling fast!
   *(Flutter fingers down
   to represent falling snow.)*
Stick your tongue out, catch a flake,
   (Catch a pretend snowflake on tongue.)
And try to make it last, hey!
   (Rub tummy.)

Lift your feet, let's all march,
Through the snow so deep,
   (Pretend to trudge through snow.)
Just be glad you're not a bear,
'Cause you'd be fast asleep!
   (Rest head on hands as if sleeping.)

Signs of Spring

Use this delightful rhyme to welcome the signs of spring.

The robin flaps her wings and tweets.

(Pretend to flap "wings.")

The rabbit hops and thumps his feet.

*(Hold up two fingers and
bounce hand.)*

The bees are buzzing 'round
and 'round,

*(Make circles in the air with
index fingers.)*

And seeds are sprouting from
the ground.

*(Slowly open fisted hands,
extending fingers upward.)*

Gentle breezes fill the air,

(Move hand in wavy line through air.)

And butterflies are everywhere.

*(Hook thumbs together and
flutter fingers.)*

These signs come only once a year—

(Hold up one finger.)

To tell the world that spring is here!

*(Hold arms out to sides,
as if to say "Ta-da!")*

What Is Summer?

Warm up to the fun days of summer with this lively action rhyme.

Summer is baseball.

(Pretend to swing baseball bat.)

Summer is heat.

(Wipe brow.)

Summer is ice cream.

(Pretend to lick ice cream cone.)

Summer's bare feet.

(Wiggle toes.)

Summer is fireworks.

(Shield eyes with both hands and look up.)

Summer is sports.

(Pretend to toss ball.)

Summer is sandy . . .

(Brush palms together to wipe of "sand.")

And always too short.

(Clasp hands to chest.)

Fall Has Come to Town

(Sing to the tune of "The Wheels on the Bus")

Sing this high-spirited song to greet the arrival of fall.

The leaves on the trees are red and brown,
> *(Hold arms in a circle over head and sway.)*

Red and brown, red and brown.

The leaves on the trees are red and brown.

Fall has come to town!

The pumpkins in the patch are big and round,
> *(Hold arms out in front to form a circle, then sway.)*

Big and round, big and round.

The pumpkins in the patch are big and round.

Fall has come to town!

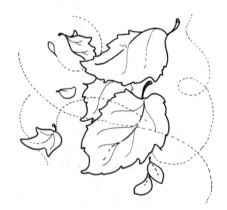

The squirrels hide their acorns in the ground,
> *(Hold up "paws" and hop in place.)*

In the ground, in the ground.

The squirrels hide their acorns in the ground.

Fall has come to town!

The leaves on the trees fall down, down, down,
> *(Raise hands, then flutter fingers downward.)*

Down, down, down, down, down, down.

The leaves on the trees fall down, down, down.

Fall has come to town!

The Wind

Perform this action rhyme to explore the playful nature of the wind.

What happens on a windy day?

(Rest chin on one hand as if thinking.)

Sometimes things just blow away.

(Reach out as if to catch something in the air.)

On your head, your hat won't stay.

(Put hands on head as if to keep a hat from blowing off.)

Clouds may seem to dance and play.

(Move arms over head in a sweeping motion.)

Tall, thin trees will bend and sway.

(Hold arms in a circle over head, then sway body.)

The wind is doing its ballet.

(Move freely and fluidly, like the wind.)

And listen—you can hear it say . . .

(Cup hand behind ear and lean forward.)

Whooooosh . . .
  Whooooosh . . .
    Whooooosh . . .

(Puff cheeks, then blow out air while whispering each "Whoosh.")

A Cloudy Day

Recite this rhyme with children for some cloudy-day fun.

A cloudy day can make you sad.

> *(Frown and trace frown with fingers.)*

Instead, it always makes me glad.

> *(Smile and trace smile with fingers.)*

Lying back, I watch the sky,

> *(Put hands behind head and look up.)*

And see amazing things go by.

> *(Sweep hand through air overhead.)*

Clouds that look like cotton cats,

> *(For each line, point to imaginary clouds overhead.)*

Clouds that look like baseball bats.

Clouds that look like rattlesnakes.

Clouds that look like birthday cakes.

I see one cloud shaped like a shark.

> *(Point to imaginary "shark" cloud.)*

Hmmm, the sky seems kind of dark . . .

> *(Stroke chin thoughtfully.)*

Hey look, that cloud looks like a plane.

> *(Point at a spot above you.)*

Whoops, I'm leaving—looks like rain!

> *(Shield brow with both hands, look up, then pretend to flip up jacket hood.)*

101 Content-Building Fingerplays, Action Rhymes, and Songs © 2009 by Pamela Chanko, Scholastic Teaching Resources

The Thunderstorm

Capture the sights, sounds, and excitement of a thunderstorm with this animated rhyme.

Pitter-patter goes the rain,
Falling from the sky,
Pitter-pitter-patter,
Like a gentle lullaby.
> *(Raise hands, then slowly lower them*
> *while wiggling fingers gently.)*

Now it comes down harder,
As it falls in heavy drops,
> *(Move hands down and*
> *wiggle fingers faster.)*

The wind is whooshing
Through the air—
The raindrops go *kerplop*!
> *(Move hands down diagonally,*
> *blowing air to represent wind.)*

And now the clouds look heavy,
And the sky is getting dark,
> *(Shield eyes with hand and look up.)*

Then here it comes,
A great big FLASH!
I just saw lightning spark!
> *(Continue shielding eyes, point up with*
> *other hand, then jump on "FLASH!")*

And what comes after lightning?
Oh, you never have to wonder . . .
> *(Squeeze eyes shut, hunch shoulders,*
> *squeeze fists, and shake with fear.)*

Just wait for it,
And soon you'll hear
A great big CLAP of thunder!
> *(Jump, pop eyes open, and*
> *clap hands together on "CLAP.")*

But lightning doesn't scare me,
And I don't mind thunderstorms . . .
> *(Put hands on hips*
> *and hold chin up in pride.)*

As long as I'm inside,
Where it is cozy,
Safe, and warm!
> *(Hug self and tuck chin into chest.)*

I'll Be Putting On My Mittens

(Sing to the tune of "She'll Be Comin' Round the Mountain")

As children sing each verse of this bouncy tune, have them pantomime putting on each article of clothing. To create additional verses, simply choose a new type of weather condition and associated clothing.

I'll be putting on my mittens if it's cold,
I'll be putting on my mittens if it's cold,
I will wrap my scarf around myself,
And then I'll zip my jacket,
Then I know I will be ready if it's cold!

I'll be putting on my rain boots if it rains,
I'll be putting on my rain boots if it rains,
I will also wear my rain hat,
Then I'll put up my umbrella,
Then I know I will be ready if it rains!

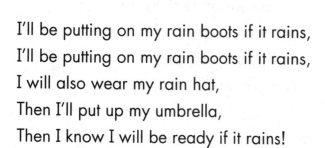

I'll be putting on my sunscreen if it's sunny,
I'll be putting on my sunscreen if it's sunny,
I will wear a floppy sunhat,
And I'll also wear dark glasses,
Then I know I will be ready if it's sunny!

From Egg to Butterfly

This fun and clever rhyme takes children through the stages of a butterfly's development.

Sitting in a leafy patch
A tiny egg's about to hatch.
(Curl up in ball on floor.)

The egg is open—what comes out?
A little critter crawls about!
(Crawl on all fours.)

That caterpillar creeps around,
And eats the leaves along the ground.
(Pretend to munch leaves.)

And then what happens? Look at this!
It spins itself a chrysalis!
(Stand, spin around once, then press arms to sides.)

Watch and wait, and one fine day
That butterfly will fly away.
(Flap arms and pretend to fly away.)

Egg-Citing Surprises

Use this riddle rhyme to help children understand that chickens aren't the only animals that hatch from eggs. At the beginning of each verse, ask children to cup their hands together to form an "egg." Then when they recite "CRRRACK," have them open their hands to "hatch" the egg. After children guess the answer to each riddle, let them act out the animal.

What grows in this egg
Is long, and it's thin.
It doesn't have legs,
But it has scaly skin.
CRRRACK!
What is it? *(Snake)*

What grows in this egg
Will be black and white.
It is a bird,
But it's never in flight.
CRRRACK!
What is it? *(Penguin)*

What grows in this egg
Will live in a swamp.
It has very sharp teeth,
And those teeth can go CHOMP!
CRRRACK!
What is it? *(Alligator)*

What grows in this egg
Is something that swims.
It breathes through its gills,
and it also has fins.
CRRRACK!
What is it? *(Fish)*

Now, inside this egg,
Something goes peck, peck, peck!
And what's coming out
Is just what you'd expect!
CRRRACK!
What is it? *(Chicken)*

101 Content-Building Fingerplays, Action Rhymes, and Songs © 2009 by Pamela Chanko, Scholastic Teaching Resources

Mamas and Babies

Children will enjoy learning the names of different baby animals with this animal rhyme.

Mama ducks have ducklings,

(Place hand below chin, then

open and close it to "quack.")

And mama seals have pups.

(Clap hands together like flippers.)

And joeys will be kangaroos,
Once they're all grown up.

(Hold up front "paws"

and bounce in place.)

Mama birds have hatchlings,

(Flap arms like wings.)

And horses have their foals.

(Pretend to ride horse by holding

"reins" and bouncing.)

Mama rabbits nurse their kits
Deep down in rabbit holes.

(Hold up two fingers and wiggle

them like rabbit ears.)

Mama pigs have piglets.

(Press thumb side of fist

to nose to make a snout.)

A cub's a bear-to-be.

(Scratch "claws" in the air.)

When my mama had a baby,

(Pretend to rock baby in arms.)

It grew up—and now it's me!

(Point to self with both thumbs.)

My Rooster

(Sing to the tune of "My Bonnie Lies Over the Ocean")

Give children a reason to crow over roosters with this irresistible song.

My rooster, he crows every morning,
*(Place hand on head with fingers raised
to represent rooster's comb.)*

He tells me the day is brand new.
*(Cross hands over head, palms facing
out, then lower arms to each side
in arc to make a rainbow.)*

My rooster is up with the sunrise,
(Hold arms in a circle over head.)

To say *cock-a-doodle-do*!
*(Tuck hands under arms
and flap elbows.)*

Wake up, wake up,
(Pretend to rub eyes.)
Just look at the sky, so blue, so blue!
(Shield eyes and look up.)

Wake up, wake up,
(Pretend to rub eyes.)
And say *cock-a-doodle*, too!
*(Tuck hands under arms
and flap elbows.)*

On the Farm

Children can use this rhyme to describe what a day on the farm might be like.

Pigs are rolling in the mud.
*(Circle fists around each other
to represent rolling.)*

Cows are chewing on their cud.
(Open and close fist.)

Crows are flying in the air.
(Extend arms and flap "wings.")

Butterflies are everywhere.
*(Hook thumbs together
and flutter fingers.)*

Mother hens sit on their eggs.
*(Tuck hands under arms
and flap "wings.")*

Little horses test their legs.
*("Walk" two fingers across arm
in wobbly motion.)*

Through the field a bunny hops,
(Bounce two fingers up and down.)

While the farmer picks his crops.
(Pretend to pick plants from ground.)

On the farm, from break of dawn,
There's always something going on!
(Hold out arms and smile.)

A Home for the Animals

Perform this rhyme with children to reinforce the types of homes that different animals live in.

A bear can live in a cave,

(Make a fist "bear" and move it into "cave" formed by other hand.)

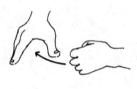

And a bunny can live in a hole.

(Make "hole" with one hand, then push "bunny ears" through hole and wiggle them.)

A robin can live in a nest,

(Cup one hand for "nest," then open and close pincher fingers on other hand to make a chirping "bird.")

And a burrow's a home for a mole.

(Make "burrow" with one hand, then slide other hand into the top of burrow.)

A web is a home for a spider,

(Spread fingers of one hand for "web," then make "spider" with pincher fingers of other hand and place on web.)

And a fish likes the sea very well.

(Hold palms down and "swim" them toward and across each other.)

A tree is a home for a squirrel,

(Hold up one arm and spread fingers to make "tree," then "crawl" two fingers up the tree.)

And a turtle just lives in its shell!

(Cover one hand with the other, extending index finger of bottom hand to represent a turtle's head.)

Way Down Deep in the Big Blue Sea

Introduce children to a few deep-sea critters with this fun fingerplay.

Way down deep in the big blue sea,

("Dive" both hands down and back up.)

An itty-bitty fishy was looking at me.

(Hold left hand up with palm facing right,

then "swim" right hand toward left hand.)

I looked right back and, as a matter of fact,

(Bend fingers of left hand up and down

to "talk" to right hand.)

That **fishy** swam away, and it never swam back!

("Swim" right hand away and put behind back.)

Repeat the rhyme, performing the same actions for each verse and replacing the boldface words in the second and fourth lines with the following:

A shiny, shiny dolphin; dolphin
A flippy-flappy seal; seal

A toothy white shark; shark
A great blue whale; whale

Playful Penguins

Children can pretend to be perky penguins when performing this lively action rhyme.

Way up north where cold winds blow,
Penguins waddle through the snow.
 (Waddle in place.)

They slip and slide along the ice;
They think the cold is rather nice.
 (Sway back and forth
 as if slipping and sliding.)

Black and white and wild and free,
They swim about the icy sea.
 (Make swimming motions.)

There's just one thing this bird won't try—
You'll never see a penguin fly!
 (Shake finger "no.")

The Days of Dinosaurs

(Sing to the tune of "When Johnny Comes Marching Home")

Reflect on the prehistoric days of earth's largest reptiles with this high-spirited tune.
Each time "Hurrah!" is sung, have children raise their fists in a cheering motion.

The dinosaurs came out to play,
Hurrah! Hurrah!
The carnivores ate meat all day,
Hurrah! Hurrah!

The herbivores ate up the plants,
Then all the dinos did a dance.
*(Raise both index fingers and pump
arms into air to indicate dancing.)*
It was long ago,
When dinosaurs walked the Earth.

Some dinosaurs had pointy backs,
Hurrah! Hurrah!
Some dinosaurs made giant tracks,
Hurrah! Hurrah!

Some dinos' necks,
    they reached so high,
You'd think that they
    could touch the sky,
    (Point up to sky.)
It was long ago,
When dinosaurs walked the Earth.

The dinosaurs were big and strong,
    (Flex biceps.)
Hurrah! Hurrah!
 But then the dinos said, "So long!"
    (Wave goodbye.)
Hurrah! Hurrah!

What happened is a mystery,
    (Shrug shoulders, palms up.)
But a dinosaur you will never see.
    (Shake head "no.")
It was long ago,
When dinosaurs walked the Earth.

From Seed to Flower

Use this rhyme to reinforce how a plant grows.

Underground, beneath the soil,
There lies a tiny seed.
   (Squat down, wrap arms around knees,
   and tuck chin into chest.)
It doesn't move or stir until
It gets just what it needs.

A little sun, a little rain,
That seed is growing roots.
   (Wiggle feet.)
A little air, then out it pops—
A tiny little shoot!
   (Raise head up and stretch neck.)

Next a little leaf grows out,
With water, light, and air.
   (Hold one hand out to side.)
The stem gets taller, then you'll see
   (Slowly rise from ground.)
A flower growing there!

The flower grows, its petals spread;
   (Keep rising, spreading both arms out.)
It's growing very tall.
   (Rise to full height and look up.)
That seed became a sunflower—
The tallest flower of all!

My Vegetable Garden

Children pick imaginary, but nutritious, garden foods with this clever rhyme.

 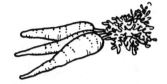

I planted some nice crunchy carrots.
Now I'm pulling them out of the ground.   *(Pretend to pull carrots out of ground.)*

I planted some leafy green lettuce.
Now it's growing in rows up and down.   *(Sweep index finger back and forth to indicate rows of plants.)*

I planted some ripe red tomatoes.
Now I'm picking them off of the vine.   *(Pretend to pick tomatoes off vine.)*

I planted some celery also.
Now it's standing straight up in a line.   *(Stand up straight, press arms to sides, and stiffen body.)*

Now I'm putting the plants in my basket,   *(Pretend to put veggies in basket.)*
And I'm washing and chopping them, too.   *(Pretend to wash and chop.)*

Can you guess what I grew in my garden?   *(Shrug shoulders, holding palms up at sides.)*
A salad for me and for you!   *(Rub tummy, point to self and then others.)*

Apples and Pumpkins

Harvest time has never been more fun than with this action rhyme!

Apples growing in a tree,

(Standing, point one finger up in the air.)

Reach up high, grab one for me!

(Reach up and pretend to pick apple.)

Pumpkins growing on a vine,

(Point down to the ground.)

Reach down low, make that one mine!

(Reach down and pretend to pick pumpkin.)

Where can apples and pumpkins be found?

(Hold palms up and shrug shoulders.)

Up in the trees . . .

(Point up in the air.)

. . . and down on the ground!

(Point down to the ground.)

Soil, Water, Air, and Light

(Sing to the tune of "Head, Shoulders, Knees, and Toes")

Children learn about the needs of plants with this action song. Each time you repeat the words from the first three lines, perform the actions indicated in the first verse. As children become more familiar with the words and movement, challenge them to perform the song over and over, singing it faster each time.

Soil,

(Crouch down with both hands on floor.)

Water,

(Rise slowly to standing while "pouring" water onto plants.)

Air and light.

(Wiggle fingers in air, then point to sun.)

Air and light.

Soil,

Water,

Air and light,

Air and light.

These things make a plant grow right,

(Crouch down, press palms together over head,

then slowly rise to standing.)

Soil,

Water,

Air and light,

Air and light!

The Forgotten Acorn

What happens to the acorns that squirrels leave behind? Children find out with this special rhyme.

Look at the squirrels,
They hop all around,

(Hold up two fingers and bend down tips to make "ears," then "hop" ears around.)

They bury their acorns
Deep under the ground.

(Form fist to make acorn, then "bury" it in other hand.)

They dig up those acorns,
All they can find—

("Dig" into air with both hands.)

But sometimes an acorn
Can get left behind.

(Form fist to make acorn, then cover with other hand to represent "ground.")

From deep underground,
It grows and it grows,

(Poke index finger of "acorn" through "ground" and slowly raise finger.)

Taller and taller,
And nobody knows

(Continue raising finger until it stands upright.)

That the beautiful oak tree
On this very spot

(Slowly raise arms.)

Came from an acorn
A squirrel forgot!

(Continue raising arms until they form a circle over head, representing a tree.)

All the Little Firefighters

Children act out the role of firefighters with this lively rhyme.

All the little firefighters, fast asleep.

(Press hands together, rest head on hands, and close eyes.)

They hear the bell, then up they leap!

(Leap up to standing position.)

They rush to put on all their gear.

(Pretend to put on boots, pants, suspenders, and hat.)

They drive their truck—the fire's near!

(Pretend to drive a fire truck.)

They grab the hose and point the spout—

(Pretend to spray water hose back and forth.)

They fight that fire 'til it's out!

(Wipe "sweat" from brow, then shake it off hand.)

And now that firetruck, big and red,

(Pretend to steer wheel.)

Takes those firefighters back to bed!

(Press hands together, rest head on hands, and close eyes.)

Police on Patrol

Use this action rhyme to teach about different ways police get around on the job.

Some police are traffic cops.
Hear that whistle? It means "Stop."

*(Pretend to blow whistle with one hand
while holding out palm of other hand
to indicate "stop.")*

Some police walk down the street.
They keep us safe while on their feet.

(March in place.)

Some police ride on a horse.
They help protect our parks, of course.

(Hold "reins" and bounce in "saddle.")

Some police ride in a car.
They help people near and far.

(Pretend to steer wheel.)

Whatever place they may be found,

(Spread arms out wide.)

Police help keep us safe and sound!

*(Wrap arms around self and twist
back and forth.)*

Something for the Letter Carrier

This rhyme delivers a bag full of appreciation for the jobs that letter carriers do.

He walks and walks from house to house,

(Pump arms as if walking.)

With letters in his sack.

(Pretend to carry sack over shoulder.)

He brings us cards and magazines,

*(Pretend to remove something from sack
and hand to someone.)*

But what does he get back?

(Frown and shrug shoulders.)

He brings our mail, he works so hard,

(Wipe "sweat" from brow, then shake it off hand.)

His sack filled to the brim.

(Hold arms out front to form a circle.)

I think I'll write a thank-you,

(Pretend to write on palm.)

And deliver it to him!

*(Press crossed palms against chest, then extend
hands forward as if giving something away.)*

The School Bus Driver

(Sing to the tune of "Here We Go 'Round the Mulberry Bush")

This cheerful song reminds children of a school bus driver's responsibilities—
and their own when riding the bus.

The school bus driver drives the bus,

(Pretend to steer wheel.)

Drives the bus, drives the bus.

The school bus driver drives the bus,

To take the kids to school.

The driver needs to watch the road,

(Shield brow with one hand, then the other.)

Watch the road, watch the road.

The driver needs to watch the road,

To take the kids to school.

The driver needs to listen up,

(Alternate cupping each ear

with each hand.)

Listen up, listen up.

The driver needs to listen up.

To take the kids to school.

You can help by sitting still,

(Sit with hands in lap.)

Sitting still, sitting still.

(Whisper this line, with finger to lips.)

This will help the school bus driver

Take the kids to school!

(Pretend to drive bus.)

At the Doctor's

Use this rhyme to ease children's anxieties about visiting the doctor.

When I go to see the doctor
She listens to my heart.
  (Tap heart with fist.)
She checks inside my ears
  (Tug earlobes.)
And she writes stuff in a chart.
  (Pretend to write on clipboard.)

She taps me with a hammer
To make my leg go "bounce,"
  (Tap knee with fist and lift calf.)
She checks to see how tall I've grown
  *(Hold one hand horizontally above
  head to indicate height.)*
And weighs me ounce by ounce!

Sometimes my doctor gives me shots,
  (Poke arm with index finger.)

Which always makes me blue.
  (Frown.)

But she cheers me up by saying
  (Smile.)

I was brave, and now I'm through!
  *(Brush hands together back and forth
  to indicate "finished.")*

Pets Need Vets!

This rhyme helps children learn how vets can help their pets.

If your puppy's got the flu,
    (Pretend to sneeze.)
Then the vet knows what to do.

If your kitten's hurt her knee,
    (Frown and rub knee.)
Then the vet's the one to see.

If your parrot's throat is sore,
    (Place hands on throat.)
Then the vet will have a cure.

If your turtle stubs his toe,
    (Frown and hold toe.)
Then the vet is where to go.

If your cow has lost her moo,
    (Cup hand behind ear, frown, and shake head.)
Then the vet can help her, too.

And if you've got so many pets,
Maybe you'll become a vet!
    (Point out.)

When I Grow Up

Children can use this fingerplay to explore the many different
careers they might choose when they grow up.

When I grow up, I'd like to be
A very famous writer.

> *(Pretend to write on palm.)*

But I am brave, so I could
Also be a firefighter.

> *(Point a pretend hose and*
>
> *move it side to side.)*

I really love to act,
So I could be a movie star.

> *(Strike a glamorous pose.)*

And I'm good at music, too,
So I could also play guitar.

> *(Pretend to strum guitar.)*

I really love to travel,
So I might conduct a train.

> *(Close fist and pretend*
>
> *to pull cord.)*

But why not travel in the air,
And also fly a plane?

> *(Hold arms out like wings*
>
> *and tilt side to side.)*

I'm very good at sports,
So I could be a baseball player.

> *(Pretend to swing baseball bat.)*

And I love to make long speeches, too,
So why not be the mayor?

> *(Lift chin and hold neck*
>
> *as if clearing throat.)*

It's a good thing that I'm very smart,
And learn so quickly, too.

> *(Tap head with index finger and smile.)*

'Cause I sure have an awful lot
Of things I want to do!

> *(Press palms to cheeks.)*

Around the Town

Use this rhyme as a guessing game; the answers are in parentheses. On the repeated refrain, have children walk their fingers around the floor or a table, and then stop for the rhyming riddle. When the riddle is answered, they can "walk around town" again.

Refrain:

What is in a busy town?

Let's take a little walk around!

This is a place where people can look

Whenever they want

To check out a good book.

Where are we? *(Library)*

Refrain

This place is good for sending a letter.

Want to buy stamps?

There's no place that's better.

Where are we? *(Post Office)*

Refrain

Here is a place for storing your pennies.

Keep putting them here,

And someday you'll have many.

Where are we? *(Bank)*

Refrain

Here is a place where children can go

To learn many things

And then show what they know.

Where are we? *(School)*

Refrain

Here is a place where people can eat.

And they don't have to cook,

Which is really a treat!

Where are we? *(Restaurant)*

101 Content-Building Fingerplays, Action Rhymes, and Songs © 2009 by Pamela Chanko, Scholastic Teaching Resources

The Playground

This playful rhyme lets children imagine the good times that await them on the playground.

Ride a seesaw
Up and down.

("Seesaw" hands up and down.)

Turn a go-round
'Round and 'round.

(Push "merry-go-round" in a circle.)

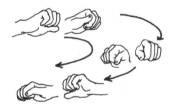

Whoosh your way
Straight down a slide.

("Slide" hand downward.)

Bounce a horse
And take a ride.

(Pretend to ride horse.)

Climb up on
The monkey bars.

(Pretend to climb.)

Swing until you
Touch the stars.

(Swing arms up and back.)

No matter what you
Like to do,

*(Hold palms up
and shrug shoulders.)*

The playground
Is the place for you!

(Point to another child.)

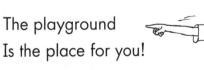

City and Country

Children compare life in the city and country with this action rhyme.

In the city there are buildings
Soaring high into the sky.

(Raise arms over head, bend hands,
and touch fingertips together
to form a rectangle.)

In the country you pick apples
For a homemade apple pie.

(Pretend to pick apple from tree.)

In the city there are busy streets
And taxicabs to hail.

(Reach out arm to "hail" taxi.)

In the country you can milk a cow,
Collect it in a pail.

(Pump fists as if milking cow.)

In the city there's a subway—
You can travel underground.

(Point down.)

In the country there are meadows
Where fresh daisies can be found.

(Pretend to pick flowers.)

In the city and the country,
There are different things to see.

(Shield eyes with one hand,
then the other.)

But one thing they have in common—
Children live there, just like me!

(Point to self.)

The Neighborhood Recycling Dance

(Sing to the tune of "The Hokey Pokey")

Stand in a circle to perform the actions to this song. You can add more verses by replacing "plastic" with other recyclable materials, such as cardboard, metal, paper, and so on.

You put the plastic in,

(Pretend to place item in circle.)

You leave the garbage out,

(Pretend to toss item out of circle.)

You put the plastic in,

(Pretend to place item in circle.)

And then something new comes out!

(Hold hands out with palms up,
as if saying "Ta-da!")

Recycle and you'll help your town,
As Earth spins 'round and 'round,

(Spin around once.)

That's what it's all about!

(Clap.)

Wheels

Have children perform the actions to this rhyme as they learn
how people get around in wheeled vehicles.

Most anywhere you want to go
Wheels can get you there, you know.
(Roll hands around each other

to indicate wheels rolling.)

Traveling just down the street?
A bicycle cannot be beat.
(Pretend to grip handlebars

and pedal with feet.)

Need to get to someplace far?
Might be best to take the car.
(Pretend to steer wheel.)

Going to a busy town?
A bus will take you all around.
(Bounce up and down in seat

and shield brow while looking around.)

Yes, anywhere you're traveling,
A set of wheels is just the thing!
(Roll hands around each other

to indicate wheels rolling.)

101 Content-Building Fingerplays, Action Rhymes, and Songs © 2009 by Pamela Chanko, Scholastic Teaching Resources

Land, Water, and Air

This rhyme teaches about the kinds of land, water, or air vehicles used by people everywhere.

Clickety-clack, clickety-clack,
A train goes chugging down the track.

(Pump arms to imitate train chugging along.)

Up, up, up, so very high,
An airplane flies across the sky.

("Fly" one hand up over head and then back down.)

Slow and steady, that's the motion
Liners use to across the ocean.

*(Hold one arm horizontally across front of body,
then form upside-down V with other hand
and glide it along arm.)*

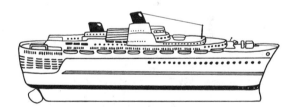

On land, on water, and in the air—

(Point left, right, then up.)

Transportation's everywhere!

(Hold arms out to sides.)

The Rocketship

Children blast off on an imaginary space adventure with this exciting action rhyme.

Climb aboard the rocketship,
It's time to fly away!
   (Make beckoning gesture.)
We're launching into outer space,
We're taking off today!
   (Point up to space.)

So let's begin the countdown,
We'll start with number ten.
   (Hold up ten fingers.)
Then after our adventure,
We'll come back to Earth again!

Ready?
   *(Crouch down, then slowly rise
   to standing while counting down.)*

Ten,
Nine,
Eight,
Seven,
Six,
Five,
Four,
Three,
Two,
One . . .

Blastoff!
*(Stretch arms straight over
head, press palms together,
then jump.)*

First Day Fever!

Use this rhyme to capture all the excitement of the first day of school.

A brand new year has just begun.
Get ready to have lots of fun!
(Clasp hands.)

We'll make new friends—
So wave hello.
(Wave.)

We'll learn new things—
There's lots to know!
(Point to head.)

We'll get to paint,
(Pretend to paint.)
We'll get to play.
(Clap.)

A new school year is here—
HOORAY!
*(Raise both arms in the air
in a cheering motion.)*

Goodbye Letters

Recite this rhyme to help children sum up the school year that's ending and to look forward to the year ahead.

G is for all of the **G**ood
times we had.

(Give two "thumbs-up" signs.)

O is for **O**ver,
Which might make us sad.

*(Frown and trace imaginary
tears down cheeks.)*

O's also for **O**lder,
'Cause all of us grew.

*(Hold hand above head
as if measuring height.)*

D is for **D**reams
That we hope will come true.

(Clasp hands at chest.)

B is for all the good **B**ooks
That we read.

*(Press palms together,
then open them like a book.)*

Y's for the **Y**ear
That's behind and ahead.

*(Point thumb over shoulder,
then point finger ahead.)*

E is for getting
A great **E**ducation.

*(Smile and tap head
with index finger.)*

And that spells **GOODBYE**—
Happy summer vacation!

(Wave goodbye.)

Birthday Bake-Off

Use this rhyme to celebrate any child's birthday. Use the birthday child's name in the first, fifth, and sixth verses and his or her age in the fifth verse to name the number of candles.

Today is _____'s birthday,
Let's make a cake!
Put on your apron,
Get ready to bake!
(Pretend to put on apron.)

Pour in some flour,
Some buttermilk, too.
("Pour" with one hand, then the other.)
Crack open an egg,
Then what do we do?
(Pretend to crack egg with both hands.)

We mix it and stir it
As hard as we can,
(Pretend to stir with both hands.)
And then pour the batter
Right into a pan.
(Pretend to pour batter.)

Put the pan in the stove,
Take it out when it's done,
*(Pretend to put pan in oven,
then take it out.)*
And then we can frost it together—
What fun!
(Pretend to frost cake.)

Put _____ candles
On top of the cake
*(Hold up number of fingers used
in the blank.)*
While _____ decides
On the best wish to make!
(Scratch head as if thinking.)

"Happy birthday to _____!"
Is what we all shout.
*(Cup hands around mouth,
as if shouting.)*
Now take a deep breath,
And blow them all out!
*(Birthday child pretends to blow out
candles as others clap.)*

Who's Who on Halloween

This reassuring rhyme reminds children that Halloween is a time of make-believe.

I never know who I might meet

(Hold palms up and shrug shoulders.)

When I go out to trick-or-treat.

(Clap.)

Witches with their pointy hats,

(Form a triangle with hands and hold it over head.)

Spooky cats and scary bats.

(Hold index fingers above head and wiggle like ears.)

Ghosts and goblins saying, "Boo,"

(Cup hands around mouth as if calling out.)

Skeletons and monsters, too.

(Wiggle fingers and make spooky face.)

But they don't frighten me, you see—

(Shake head.)

'Cause underneath, they're kids like me!

(Point to self.)

A Week of Adventures

Celebrate National Children's Book Week with this imaginative rhyme.

Today I saw a dinosaur,
Just walking down the road.
(Pound fists on floor or table
to imitate heavy footsteps.)
I also saw a princess
As she kissed a tiny toad.
(Pretend to hold toad in one hand,
and blow kiss with other hand.)

Next, I met an alligator,
Crying salty tears.
(Frown and trace imaginary tears
rolling down cheeks.)
Later, I'll go back in time
A hundred million years.
(Point both thumbs back over shoulders.)

Tomorrow I will go to space,
And bounce around the moon.
(Point up, then bounce up and down.)
My picnic with the Queen can wait
'Til Tuesday afternoon.
(Extend pinky to sip from imaginary
teacup, then shrug shoulders.)

I know you don't believe me.
I can see it in your look.
(Squint, put one hand on hip,
and shake finger of other hand.)
But it's true, and you can do it, too—
(Smile and point to others.)
By opening a book!
(Press palms together,
then open them like a book.)

Help on Thanksgiving

Use this clever rhyme to get children geared up to be Thanksgiving helpers.

I'm a holiday helper,
And I help with many things.
(Point thumb to self.)

I help to set the table,
Putting napkins in their rings.
(Form circle with one hand,
then poke fingers of other hand in circle.)

I help to do the dishes—
I can wash, and I can dry.
(Pretend to wash dishes.)

I help roll out the crust
To make a yummy pumpkin pie.
(Pretend to roll dough with rolling pin.)

I help to mash potatoes,
And I help to stir the stew.
(Pretend to mash, then stir with spoon.)

I help a lot with dinner—
And I help to eat it, too!
(Rub tummy.)

101 Content-Building Fingerplays, Action Rhymes, and Songs © 2009 by Pamela Chanko, Scholastic Teaching Resources

Holidays, Celebrations & Special Times

The Perfect Present

Encourage children to recite this special rhyme anytime they
want to give a loved one a perfect gift for the winter holidays.

There's a present I can give,
And it doesn't cost a dime.
   (Shake finger "no.")

It's good for winter holidays,
Or any special time.
   (Put hands on heart.)

I never need to wrap it up,
Or tie it with a bow.
   (Shake head, pretend to tie bow.)

It's great for friends and family,
And everyone I know.
   (Spread arms wide.)

So if you want a present,
Or even two or three,
   (Hold up two fingers, then three.)

Just ask, and you will get your gift—
A great big hug from me!
   (Hug self.)

New Year's Countdown

Greet the new year with this cheery countdown rhyme.

It's almost midnight, give a cheer

(Raise fists in cheering motion.)

We're ringing in a brand new year!

(Pretend to ring bell.)

Everybody watch the clock,

(Shield brow with hand.)

Hear it tick and hear it tock!

(Cup hand behind ear.)

It's so exciting, we can't wait—

(Clap hands)

That is why we're up so late!

(Tap wrist as if touching watch.)

People shout all over town—

(Cup hands around mouth.)

Listen, hear them counting down!

*(Point to ears, then hold up ten fingers.
Fold down one finger at a time
while counting down.)*

Ten!

Nine!

Eight!

Seven!

Six!

Five!

Four!

Three!

Two!

One!

HAPPY NEW YEAR!

(Jump up and cheer.)

Happy Birthday, Dr. King

Perform this rhyme while sitting or standing in a circle,
so that children can join hands at the end.

A man once had a special dream,
His name was Dr. King.   *(Rest chin on clasped hands.)*
He dreamed of peace and harmony.
He said, "Let freedom ring."   *(Spread arms out wide.)*

He dreamed that people everywhere
Would stand up tall and proud.   *(Put hands on hips and throw shoulders back.)*
He dreamed we all could get along,
He said it right out loud.   *(Raise fist in cheering motion.)*

We can make his dream come true
By being kind and fair,   *(Clasp hands together and nod.)*
By showing our respect and love
For people everywhere.   *(Press hands to heart,*

                                          then spread arms out to sides.)

His birthday is a special day—
We all join hands and sing.   *(Join hands and sway.)*
For there's no nicer way to say,
"We love you, Dr. King!"

What's Up, Groundhog?

Teach children this fingerplay to perform on Groundhog Day.

Groundhog, groundhog, underground,

(Make a fist with right hand,

then cover it with left hand.)

Please pop up and look around.

(Poke index finger of fist through

fingers of left hand.)

See a shadow by your door,

(Hold right index finger straight up and left

index finger parallel to ground.)

And winter's here for six weeks more.

(Shiver body while holding hands in place.)

But if you see no shadow there,

(Curl left finger in.)

It means that spring is in the air!

(Open hands and spread out to sides

to form rainbow.)

Making a Valentine

Children can present this sweet Valentine rhyme to their loved ones over and over again.

I'm cutting out a great big heart.

(Make "scissors" with two fingers, then pretend to cut.)

I'm squeezing on some glue.

(Pretend to squeeze glue onto paper.)

I'm writing out a message—

(Pretend to write.)

It's a Valentine for you!

(Point out.)

My Valentine has words to read,

(Pretend to track print with finger.)

And fuzzy felt to touch.

(Softly rub fingertips across back of opposite hand.)

"I love you," says my Valentine,

(Put hands over heart.)

But words can't say how much!

(Spread arms out wide.)

100th Day Quiz

Celebrate the 100th day of school with this humorous rhyme.

Do you think it would be nice
To have 100 mice?

*(Wiggle index fingers above head
like mouse ears.)*

Do you think it would be funny
To have 100 bunnies?

*(Hold up two fingers
and bounce them up and down.)*

Do you think it would be grand
To have 100 hands?

(Wave both hands.)

Do you think it would be neat
To have 100 feet?

(Wiggle both feet.)

Do you think it would be dishy
To have 100 fishies?

*(Press palms together and zig-zag them
in swimming motion.)*

Do you think it would be funky
To have 100 monkeys?

*(Raise one arm and pretend
to scratch armpit with other hand.)*

For monkeys, mice, and such,
We think 100 is too much!

*(Shake head and hold palms out
in "stop" gesture.)*

But we think it's really cool
We've had 100 days of school!

(Give two "thumbs-up" signs.)

Presidents on Parade

Remember two great men on Presidents' Day with this special fingerplay.

On Presidents' Day, the people
Of our country celebrate.

(Raise fist in cheering motion.)

We celebrate the birthdays
Of two leaders who were great.

(Hold up two fingers.)

Lincoln was the president
Who wore the tall black hat.

(Pretend to tip hat.)

His face is on the penny,
But his worth was more than that!

*(Make small circle with
index finger and thumb.)*

Washington, our country's first,
Was very wise and brave.

*(Tap index finger on head, then put
hands on hips and puff up chest.)*

You'll see this leader's face
On every quarter that you save.

*(Make medium-sized circle with
middle finger and thumb.)*

Being a great president
Is very hard to do.

(Raise hand in salute and nod.)

But Abe and George both did it—
And someday, so may you!

(Point out.)

I'm a Little Leprechaun

(Sing to the tune of "I'm a Little Teapot")

Children will enjoy singing this bouncy tune to commemorate St. Patrick's Day.

I'm a little leprechaun,

   (Pinch thumb and index finger together.)

Short and cute.

   (Gently poke index finger into cheek.)

Here is my hat,

   (Pretend to tip hat.)

And here are my boots.

   (Point to feet.)

If you follow me

   (Make beckoning gesture.)

In my bright green suit,

   (Pretend to put thumbs under jacket lapels.)

A pot of gold will be your loot!

   (Hold arms out in front to form a circle,

   as if carrying a large pot.)

Earth Day Gifts

With this fingerplay, children learn about Earth's gifts to them—and how they can give to Earth in return.

Big tall trees,

(Hold out arms to represent tree branches.)

A sky of blue,

(Point up to sky.)

These are gifts Earth gives to you.

(Press crossed palms against chest, then extend

hands forward as if giving something away.)

A shining sun,

(Raise arms above head to form circle.)

An ocean deep,

(Make wavy motion with hand.)

Earth says these are yours to keep.

(Clasp hands to chest.)

And though these gifts
From Earth are free,
We must take care of them, you see.

(Raise index finger.)

Help to keep these gifts like new,
And you give Earth
A present, too!

(Extend arms forward with palms up.)

Fantastic Fireworks!

For this Independence Day rhyme, let children be the fireworks! Have them spread out so each child has plenty of room to move. Then, on each capitalized sound word, let children jump, kick, leap, and "explode" in any way they like.

Today's the day for fireworks—
Stand back and give them room!
Look! Look up! Up in the sky!
I think I see . . .

KABOOM!

Today's the day we show our pride
For good old Uncle Sam.
Oh wait, here comes another one,
Exploding with a . . .

BAM!

Today we celebrate the day
When bells of freedom rang.
We wave the flag, we have parades—
Oh look, here comes a . . .

BANG!

Fireworks are how we say
We love the U.S.A.
They're very, very noisy,
And they make us shout . . .

HOORAY!